RIDDLE GIGGLES

RIDDLE GIGGLES

by HELEN HOKE

Pictures by TONY PARKHOUSE

FRANKLIN WATTS, INC.
New York, N.Y.
1975

First published in Great Britain by Franklin Watts, Ltd., London

First American publication by Franklin Watts, Inc., New York

Copyright © 1975 by Franklin Watts Limited

All rights reserved

ISBN 0-531-02096-7

Library of Congress Catalog Number 74-26364

Printed in Great Britain

RIDDLE GIGGLES

RIDDLE RIGHT ON!

Why was the poor dog chasing his tail?

He was trying to make both ends meet.

How is a nursery like a dance hall?

It's a bawlroom.

Why did the old lady who lived in a shoe buy her children a dachshund?

So that they could all pat him at the same time.

Why can't the little boy play on the piano?

Because he can't climb that high.

How did Mrs. Manybride become a bill collector?

All her husbands were named William.

Why was the sick boy about to croak?

He swallowed a frog.

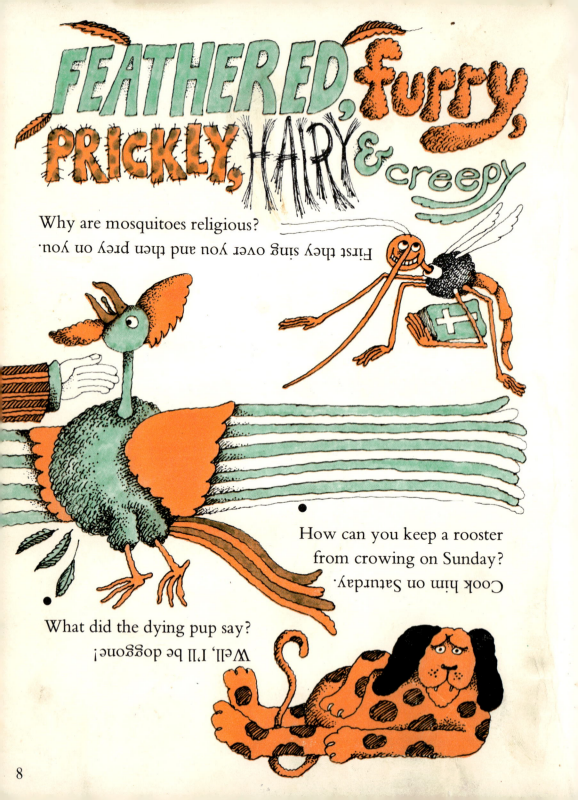

FEATHERED, furry, PRICKLY, HAIRY, & creepy

Why are mosquitoes religious?

First they sing over you and then they prey on you.

How can you keep a rooster from crowing on Sunday?

Cook him on Saturday.

What did the dying pup say?

Well, I'll be doggone!

For what reason did the chicken cross the road?

For its own fowl reasons.

What insects are the happiest?

Mosquitoes: they sing at their work.

Why does a moth lead such an awful life?

It spends the hot summer in a fur coat, and the freezing
winter in a bathing suit.

9

RIDDLES TO FLEA FROM!

What did the two old fleas do when they retired?

They bought themselves a dog and went to live at the seaside.

Why did the organist give up his musical career?

His monkey died.

What kind of cat do you always find in a library?

A cat-alogue.

What's one of the best things a rooster has to offer?

Hentertainment.

How can you catch a monkey?

Hang upside down in a tree and act like a banana.

What is most like a hen stealin'?

A cock robin.

What's a good way to get wild duck?

Buy a tame one and annoy it.

What is a prickly pear?

Two porcupines.

Why does a bear wear a fur coat?

Because it would look absolutely silly in a raincoat.

HEART-Y RIDDLES

What kind of woman can make a man give her the shirt off his back?

A laundress.

What did the ram say to his girlfriend?

"I love ewe!"

Why did the hero refuse to die for his sweetheart?

Because his was an undying love.

12

Did the rooster really fall in love with the hen at first sight?

Well, no—she egged him on a bit.

Why did the heiress's suitor not win her hand?

He didn't suit her.

What is the state of matrimony?

One of the United States.

Why was Solomon so in love with his 999th wife?

She was one in a thousand.

FUNNY MONEY

Why didn't the pretty girl pay her taxes with a smile?

Because the tax collector insisted on cash.

Why did the poor man help his wife with the diapers?

It was a good way to make a little change.

What are assets?

Little donkeys.

14

What was the lawyer's wife called?

Sue

What is the difference between a goofy hare and a counterfeit coin?

One is a mad bunny, and the other is bad money.

Why aren't monkeys rich?

Because what they get is mostly peanuts.

What kind of robbery sounds easiest?

A safe robbery.

How does one get onto something there's a lot of money in?

Climb up to the roof of a bank.

Why was the pretty girl no longer a golddigger?

She found out about platinum.

Why does the man call himself a dynamo?

Because everything he has on is charged.

Why is a manicurist sure to get rich?

Because she makes money hand over fist.

RELATIVE RIDDLES

- What does the word "minimum" mean?

  A very small mother.

- Why did the little boy sometimes skip saying his prayers?

  Because some nights he didn't want anything.

- Why did the boy send a telegram
of congratulations to his mother?

  It was his birthday.

- What prince is every new baby boy?

  The prince of wails.

What did the boy, in Egypt long ago, say when his mother was buried?

"Goodbye, Mummy."

If a boy ate his father and mother, what would that make him?

An orphan.

Two people are standing on a bridge: one is the father of the other's son. What relation are the two people?

Husband and wife.

Why didn't the boy take the bus home?

He knew his mother would only make him take it back.

Why did the boy wear two suits to the fancy dress party?

He went as twins.

Why did the cookie cry?

Because its mother had been a wafer so long.

Why did Sleepy Sam throw away
the alarm clock?

It kept going off when he was asleep.

19

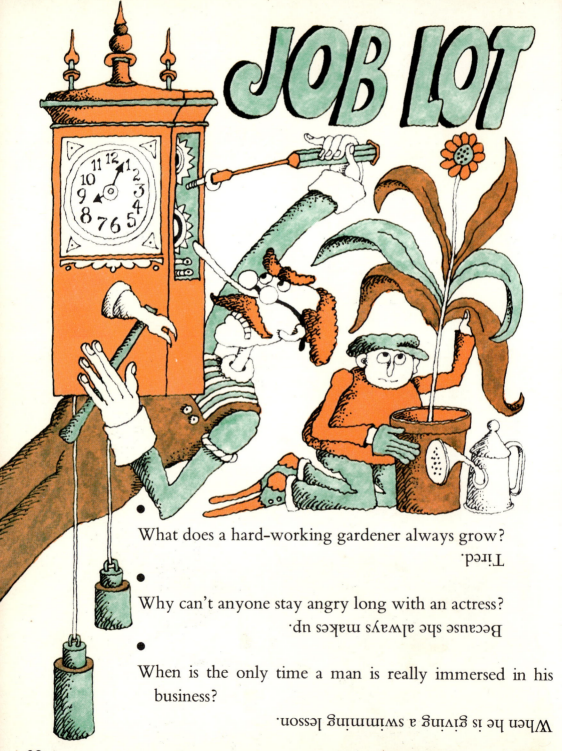

JOB LOT

- What does a hard-working gardener always grow?

  Tired.

- Why can't anyone stay angry long with an actress?

  Because she always makes up.

- When is the only time a man is really immersed in his business?

  When he is giving a swimming lesson.

What bread is better for an actor?

Better a small role than a long loaf.

What similar work do both a milkmaid and a seagull do?

One skims milk, and the other skims water.

If twelve makes a dozen, how many make a million?

Very few!

WORK WANGLES

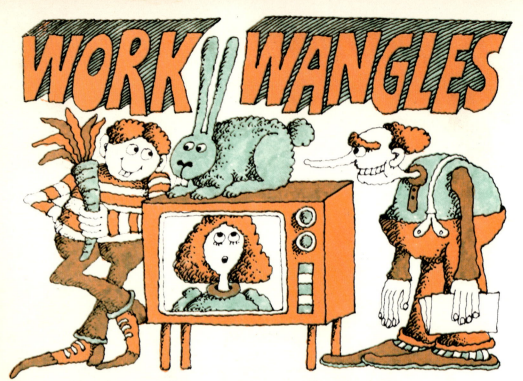

Why did the boy keep his pet rabbit in the house?

It was an ingrown hair.

When should any pig be able to write?

When he is turned into a pen.

What is the difference between an undersized witch and a deer trying to escape from a hunter?

One is a stunted hag, and the other is a hunted stag.

TEACHER: The word "madam" is spelled the same, forward and backwards: can you tell me another like it?

SMART ALEC (*casually*): Tut, tut, madam!

•

What did the stag say to his children?

"Hurry up, deer!"

•

Where does Thursday come before Wednesday?

In a dictionary.

•

What did one ram say sternly to the other, who ran, pushing ahead at the gate?

"After ewe, sir!"

23

Conundral Catchwords

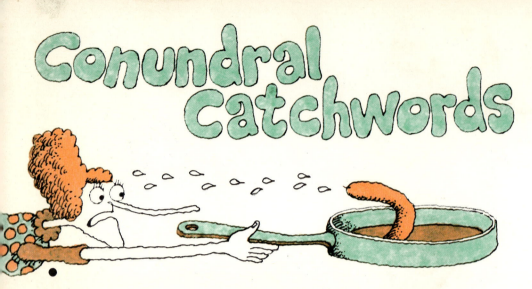

- How do you know that a sausage doesn't like being fried?

  Because it spits.

- How can one tell that coconut juice is crazy?

  It lives in a padded shell.

- Why should you always remain calm when you meet cannibals?

  In order not to get into a stew.

Why did Mrs. Newrich buy a valuable Ming vase?

Because it went so well with her ming coat.

Why is a theater such a sad place?

Because the seats are always in tiers.

What did the piece of wood say to the electric drill?

"You bore me."

Why is a woman's belt like a garbage truck?

Because it goes round and gathers the waist.

What makes a tree noisy?

Its bark.

25

ENIGMATIC EXTRAS

What is worse than being with a fool?

Fooling with a bee.

When does a man have a pinched look?

When he's riding in a patrol wagon.

What are a baby monster's parents called?

Dead and Mummy.

Why couldn't the boy sleep in class?

The teacher talked too loudly.

Why does the giraffe have such a long neck?

Because its head is so far from its body.

Why did Mother take the ink
away from the baby?

She knew he was too young to write a book.

Why did Buster give one of the new boys
next door a black eye?

They were identical twins, and he wanted
some way to tell them apart.

Why should you tickle a mule?

You might get a big kick out of it.

Why did the boy put his hands in the alphabet soup?

He was groping for words.

What would happen if you mated
an elephant with a kangaroo?

There would be big holes all over Australia.

RIDDLE GRIDDLE

Why wouldn't the man eat an apple?

His uncle died of apple-plexy.

What do porcupines have for dinner?

Prickled onions.

Why did the greedy boy pick all the white meat off the chicken?

To make a clean breast of it.

When was beef the highest it has ever been?

When the cow jumped over the moon.

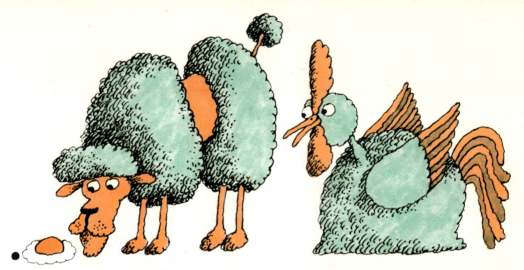

What would happen if you mated a chicken with a poodle?

The chicken would lay pooched eggs.

What soup is especially bad before taking an exam?

Noodle soup.

What do baby apes sleep in?

Apricots.

Who invented the hole in the doughnut?

Probably some silly fresh air fiend.

What's a quick lunch for a cannibal?

A sandwich-man.

Why was the chicken so tough?

It was a Plymouth Rock.

What part of a watch is used at meals?

Crystal.

Why did the steak look awful?

It was smothered with onions.

Why did the waiter keep his thumb on the steak?

He didn't want it to slide off the plate again.

What part of a fish weighs the most?

The scales.

What is the very best skin food?

Sausages, of course.

What are three popular kinds of nuts?

Peanuts, walnuts and forget-me-nuts.

Why is a pig unique?

Because you first kill him and then cure him.

Why is a baker like a beggar?

He kneads bread.

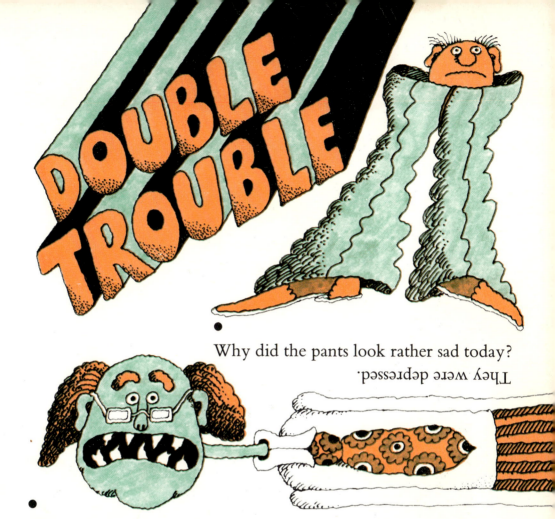

DOUBLE TROUBLE

• Why did the pants look rather sad today?

They were depressed.

• Why did the man with a peculiar voice have unnatural teeth?

He had a falsetto voice, and a false set o' teeth.

• What is the difference between a postage stamp and a girl?

One is a mail fee, and the other a female.

• What is the difference between a church bell and a thief?

One peals from the steeple, and the other steals from the people.

finny fare

What fish makes a good sandwich?

Jellyfish.

How do you get in touch with a fish?

Just drop him a line.

Why is a sardine like a cemetery?

Because it is full of bones.

How can you tell that fishes are musical?

Everyone knows about the piano tuna.

34

EXTRANEOUS MISCELLANEOUS

TEACHER, *teaching the alphabet*: Now, what comes after "O"?

BRIGHT BENNY: Yeah.

- Is it possible for a man to marry his widow's sister?

  No, because he'd be dead.

- If a class has a head and a foot, what's in between?

  The student body.

- What animal is on every legal document?

  A seal.

Why did the museum director hang the picture?

Because he couldn't find the artist.

What is a myth?

A woman who hasn't got a husband.

Why wouldn't the teacher help the boy with a problem?

She didn't think it would be right.

Why was the short-sighted girl nearly crazy with worry?

She'd lost her glasses and couldn't look for them until she found them.

Doctoral Dilemmas

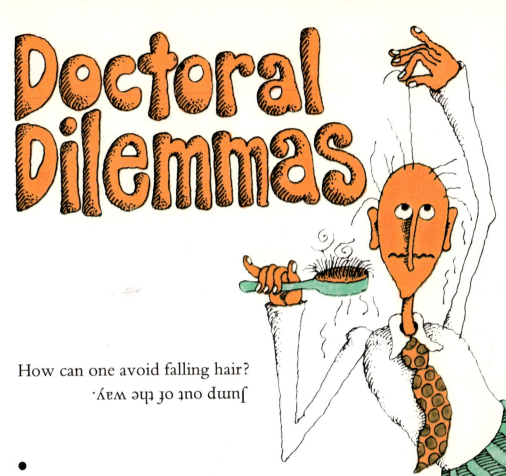

How can one avoid falling hair?

Jump out of the way.

How could you say in one word that you had been introduced to a doctor?

Metaphysician.

What should you do for a nervous friend who's all unstrung?

Send him a wire.

● When can you tell that someone has a glass eye?

When it comes out in conversation.

● If a doctor fell into a well, what *should* he have done instead?

He should have attended only to the sick, and let the well alone.

Why is a doctor a very stingy man?

Because he's supposed to treat you—and then he makes you pay for it!

Why did the old man lose his hair?

Worrying about losing his hair.

Why did the man laugh all through his operation?

The doctor put him in stitches.

TONAL TUMULT

Why would a squeaking shoe be a good songwriter?

It has music in its sole.

Why did the next-door neighbours borrow Swinging Sam's hi-fi set?

They wanted some sleep.

What pets make exciting music?

Trumpets.

Why would a drummer in a swing band make a good policeman?

Because he's used to pounding a beat.

THESE WILL DRIVE YOU NUTS

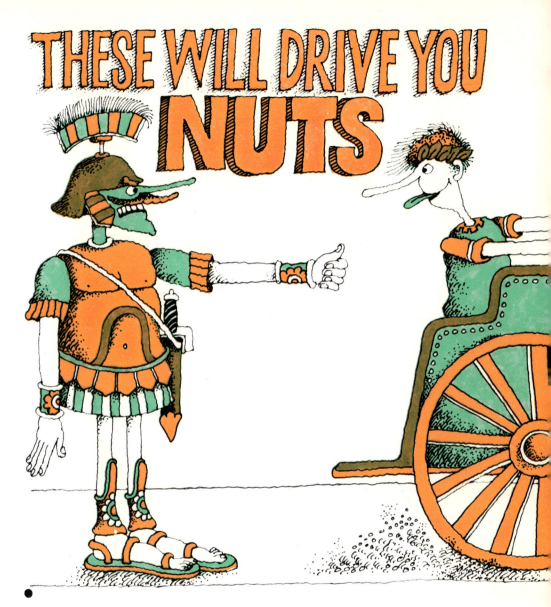

Why did the Romans build straight roads?

Because they didn't want to drive their horses round the bend.

Which driver never commits a traffic offense?

A screwdriver.

•

Why is any new baby like an up-to-date car?

Because he's a this-year's model.

•

Why did the chauffeur never have any trouble with "back-seat" drivers?

He drove a hearse.

What is a good name for the wife of an engineer?

Bridget.

Why did the boy fall in love with the snobbish girl?

It was love at first slight.

Why is a forger a very moral person?

He is always ready to write a wrong.

Why was the butcher an awkward fellow?

His hands were always in his weigh.

43

PUNNILY FUNNY

What is the difference between a pen and a pencil?

You push a pen : a pencil has to be led (lead).

Why did the cleaning woman stop cleaning?

Because she found grime doesn't pay.

Why would children everywhere object to the absence of Santa Claus?

Because they prefer his presence (presents).

TRAVEL TEASERS

- What is the equator?

  A menagerie lion running around the earth.

- What is the cheapest way to get to France?

  Be born there.

- Why is a bald man's head like Alaska?

  It's a great white bear place.

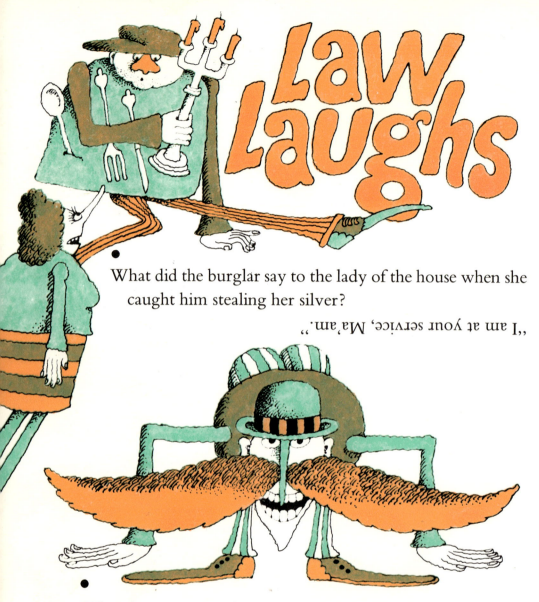

Law Laughs

- What did the burglar say to the lady of the house when she caught him stealing her silver?

"I am at your service, Ma'am."

- What does a moustache do for a man who seldom tells the truth?

It keeps him from being a really bare-faced liar.

- Why do they call it a libel suit?

Because you're liable to win and you're liable to lose.

farewell flips

- When is a healthy new baby not the usual delicate pink?

  When he's a robust yeller.

- Why will the radio never take the place of newspapers?

  You can't start a fire with a radio.

- What does a garden say when it laughs?

  "Hoe, hoe, hoe!"

- What is the easiest way to teach a parrot to talk?

  Teach it only polly-syllables.

47

●

When was the boy twins?

In a picture his mother took when he was two.

●

When is it socially correct to serve milk in a saucer?

When you feed a cat.

●

What is striped and goes round and round?

A zebra in a revolving door.

●

What did the city commuter miss most, living out in the country?

The last train home at night.